(hoosing joy, followed to all ends,
    Winding turns, escaping but never.

(hoosing joy, every ounce of soul,
    To reap passion, O' bliss of mine.

(hoosing joy, lest I want,
    The sorrow belies, O' fortress of mine.

T he wall befriends, the child cries;
    Daffodils rejoice, it's all the same.

W hen will we.. We choose joy.

Neal Harris

Pocket Stress Manager. Copyright © 1995 by Neal Harris, all rights reserved. Printed in the United States of America. No part of this book may be used or reproduced in any manner whatsoever without written permission except in the case of brief quotations embodied in critical articles and reviews. For information address CSM Publishers, P.O. Box 346, Fox River Grove, Illinois 60021

First published in 1995.

Library of Congress Cataloging-in-Publication-Data

Harris, Neal

Pocket Stress Manager ISBN 0-9649751-0-6

1. Breathing, Relaxation & Self-Enrichment
   Exercises I. Title.

AUTHOR'S NOTE

The techniques found in this book can be effective in reducing the severity of many physical and mental conditions. This book is not to take the place of proper medical or psychological treatments. If you are in doubt as to whether you can safely perform any of these techniques, due to a physical or mental difficulty, you are urged to discuss this with a professional.

This book was developed as your clear and concise guide into the realm of Relaxation and Self-Enrichment techniques. It is meant to be a practice guide, not a theoretical expedition.

The print is large, the concepts are straight-forward, and the exercises are easily learned. They have been taught successfully to thousands of people over this author's 26 years of experience.

Moreover, these techniques are simple, fast and very effective for relaxing your mind and body. In the stillness of relaxation, your mind, body and spirit are nurtured.

ACKNOWLEDGMENTS

My thanks go to my parents, Dr. Lou and Marcya, who set my feet upon this road at a young age, and who have continued to support and give value to my learning and teaching throughout their lives. I'd also like to thank my wife, Mary, whose love, vision and encouragement have seen me through this and other projects.

A big thanks to Glen Shalton for the many hours of editing and input. I would also like to thank Kaye and Sam Cooke for their considerable feedback (and Nathan and Diane Cooke for allowing their parents the time to work on this project).

Finally, there have been several mentors along the way that I would like to mention and give thanks to. They have come at opportune times in my life, and without their guidance, my attention would have undoubtedly turned to other fields of endeavor. They are: Eve Klingman, Ray Moser, Lee Wayne, Joe Scardinia, H.W.L. Poonja, and Jerry Rothermel.

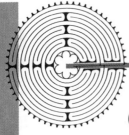

CONTENTS

Introduction

Suggested Reading

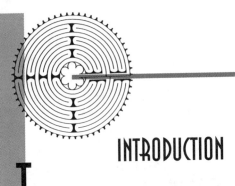

INTRODUCTION

There come times in everyone's life the realization that to move forward with professional or personal goals, the decision to change must be made. If we pay attention, we see these occurring with great frequency in the course of our lifespan; those forks in the road that provide us with choices.

The problem is that most of us are often unaware of these opportunities for change because we are on automatic pilot, a state whereby we follow well-worn patterns of basic behavior without giving them much thought or intention. This allows our thoughts to drift into the past or the future, which disables our ability to learn from the activity in the present moment. In order for personal change to occur, (like learning new ways to manage stress) we must get off automatic pilot and give ourselves ample opportunity to learn. We do this by paying attention to our circumstances from one moment to the next. Two examples of this would be tying our shoelaces and driving cars.

If you were like me, when first learning to perform each of these multi-step tasks, you probably felt some degree of nervousness, and looked at these tasks as demanding and complicated. Probably most of your attention and intention was given to performing these tasks adequately. As adults, we now see these tasks are expected and commonplace in our society, and if you answer honestly, few of us put more than just a passing thought on these activities while engaged in them.

However after surgery, a heart attack, a stroke or the process of living with cancer, people have told me that even the simplest of tasks may need to be relearned as a result of new physical or mental limitations. You can bet that for these people, learning again to tie a shoe or drive a car will require their full attention as they work hard to change these complicated tasks into habits and return to the security of being on automatic pilot.

The intention of this concise "how-to" manual is to assist you in deliberately changing the way your mind and body respond to stress, before you may be forced to examine this issue because of mental or physical difficulties. My hope is that you find this guide simple to use and effective enough to practice the techniques found within it.

For best results, practice each of these techniques 4 or 5 times before deciding which ones you can simply and effectively incorporate into your lifestyle. You can always return to the more demanding practices later.

You will notice that after each exercise, there is an "indications" section. This section gives you a list of symptoms or health concerns that have been reduced by practicing the particular technique.

Keep in mind that the contents of this book, are the culmination of my experience of practicing and teaching relaxation techniques for many years. Therefore, I don't want you to believe anything that you read in this book.

Through practice, you will find your own truths and be very capable of modifying these practices to fit your lifestyle, especially as you share your knowledge about them with others.

Some of these practices have modern and well-known origins, such as the Relaxation Response which came out of Harvard University in 1968. Others have their roots in the ancient worlds of the Far and Middle East. In total, all of these techniques are ageless in their application to the management of stress and personal development, and therefore are just as powerful in our modern world as they were in bygone eras.

My best wishes go with those of you who are embarking on this road for the first time. Your journey will be most memorable. It will require considerable patience and dedication. To others of you who are "veterans" on this road of self-learning, I am pleased to take part in your continued growth and development.

Neal Harris

CHAPTER 1

ABDOMINAL
BREATHING

Guiding Principle: When experiencing excessive or prolonged episodes of stress, our muscles have a tendency to tighten, and our reasoning/problem solving ability diminishes due to a lack of fresh oxygen. We may then tend to say and do things that we quickly regret.

Note This principle applies to all three breathing techniques which follow.

Place one hand above and one below your navel. Now take in a slow deep breath through your nose and cause your stomach area to inflate like a balloon. When you

1

have inflated the "balloon" to its greatest extent, hold your breath to a slow count of 4. Now release the breath slowly by letting it drift out between your pursed lips (as if whistling, but only hear the sound of escaping air). On the exhale, count slowly to 4, as the stomach area deflates back to normal. After several breaths, when you have felt your stomach area inflating and deflating several times, you can remove your hands and continue the breathing.

Practice Time: 1-2 minutes/session, as often as you feel the need.

Indications: Insomnia, Anxiety, Anger, Muscular Tension, High Blood Pressure, Fatigue and Asthma.

Best Time To Use: When starting to feel uncomfortable (nervous, anxious, etc.) in you car, while participating in a stressful interaction, before giving a public presentation, before going to sleep or after awakening and having difficulty returning to sleep.

DIAPHRAGMATIC
BREATHING

Hold each side of your lower ribcage with each hand.
Breathe in through your nose and imagine and feel your
ribcage expanding out against each hand.   Without
holding your breath (at the end of this natural and
relaxed inhale), exhale, while imagining and feeling your
ribcage returning to its original, resting position.

*Note: ideally, both the abdomen and chest should
remain relatively still during this breathing.*

Practice Time: 1-2 minutes/session as often as you feel
the need.

Indications: Insomnia, Anxiety, Anger,
Muscular Tension, High Blood Pressure, Fatigue.

Best Time To Use: When you start to feel uncomfortable (nervous, anxious, etc.) while participating in a

stressful interaction, before giving a public presentation, before going to sleep or after awakening and having difficulty returning to sleep.

COMPLETE BREATH

Take an Abdominal Breath as above, but this time, when you get to the end of your inhalation and your stomach area is almost completely inflated, continue inhaling by causing the middle and upper chest to inflate while the abdominal area deflates. Hold your breath and slowly count to 4. As you start to exhale, and slowly let the air out of your chest, you cause your abdomen to again inflate. Through continued exhalation, cause the abdomen to deflate and return to its relaxed position.

Practice Time: 1-2 minutes/session.

Indications: Same as Abdominal and Diaphragmatic Breathing, however it can be quicker and more effective than these when you have uncontrollable thoughts and bodily reactions, such as when you nearly avoid getting into a car accident.

Best Time To Use: When either Abdominal or Diaphragmatic Breathing doesn't bring you back to a relaxed, comfortable feeling in your mind and body.

RACHAEL'S PANIC

Rachael, a 33-year-old housewife and mother of four (all under age 6) complained of regular and violent panic attacks. She would often require her husband to take her to the nearest hospital's emergency room for relief-giving medicines. Due to thoughts racing through her head at breakneck speeds, she was unaware of the thoughts that brought on these attacks. Rachael was desperate to find any answer to these attacks other than taking tranquilizers as she feared becoming groggy at a time when her children might need her most. She was shown various breathing techniques and felt most comfortable with Abdominal Breathing. Diligently practicing this breathing technique whenever she thought of it, Rachael reported that just in that week, her thoughts had slowed down and were now less scattered. She was then able to notice the thoughts that brought on the panic attacks, and through the breathing, was able to avert the attacks before they overtook her. She realized a level of control over her mind and body that she never knew was possible. Rachael continues to practice various relaxation techniques and has discontinued all tranquilizers.

RELAXATION RESPONSE

Dr. Herbert Benson, Harvard Medical School 1968.

Guiding Principle: Positive physiological changes in the body occur through the silent, mental repetition of a relaxing word or phrase; heartbeat and respiration slow down, need for oxygen decreases, blood pressure and blood sugar are reduced and, over time, there is a decrease in the rate of physical aging as the metabolism slows down.

Breathe comfortably and naturally. Each time you feel the natural need to exhale, say to yourself the word "peace" or see the word peace in your mind's eye as you continue to breathe comfortably and naturally.

*Note other words or phrases can be substituted for the word "peace," whatever you find most relaxing, e.g. "love," "relax," "God," etc.

Practice Time: 1-2 minutes/session or until you feel comfortable again.

Indications: High Blood Pressure, high respiration rate, reducing the need for oxygen, uncontrolled Blood Sugar, changing brainwave patterns from alert beta wave activity to more relaxed and creative alpha activity.

Best Time To Use: In your car, sitting at a workstation, on a bus/train, before sleep, directly following any of the prior breathing techniques.

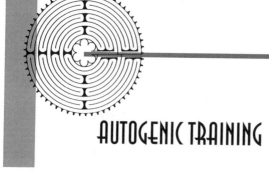

AUTOGENIC TRAINING

Dr. Johannes Schultz & Oskar Vogt, Berlin 1932.

Guiding Principle: Through the pictures we create with our minds, we can directly influence various bodily responses toward renewed health and relaxation.

Sit or lie comfortably, and begin by repeating this phrase slowly to yourself, "My hands are warm, relaxed and warm." As you do, imagine that you are lying on a beach on a warm summer day with your hands immersed in the very warm sand. Feel the sunlight shining down upon you and warming your whole body, as you continue to repeat to yourself, "My hands are warm, relaxed and

9

warm." As you feel your hands getting warmer imagine or cause that warmth to spread to any part of your body where you are feeling pain, discomfort or tension. Really focus the warmth in that area. For example if your neck is stiff or painful you might say to yourself, "My neck is warm, relaxed and warm," while focusing that warm feeling in your neck area, and so on. Feel the relief this warmth brings with it. Then, when you are ready, take in a slow, big deep breath; as you exhale, gently open your eyes.

Practice Time: 1-2 minutes/session.

Indications: Muscular tension, Headaches, High Blood Pressure, Irritable Bowel, Ulcers, Nervous Stomach.

Best Time To Use: In a quiet place, anytime of the day or night.

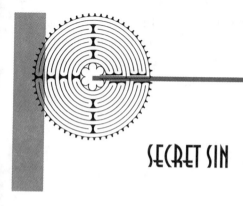

CHAPTER 4

SECRET SIN

Guiding Principle: The emotions connected to nagging situations from the past are unnecessary and detrimental to enjoying life in the present. It is possible to remember and learn from the past without dredging up painful feelings.

Write down on a small sheet of paper a brief description of a situation where you wished you would have said or done something differently. Whenever you think of this situation, you get angry at the way you handled it. It could be a situation with a family member, a friend or even a stranger.

After writing it down imagine that a close friend or family member wrote this situation about his or her own life and brought it to you to discuss. Ask yourself, "Would I hold this situation against that individual, or think them any less of a person for being involved in that situation?" If you answered "no," go on to the next paragraph. If you answered "yes," choose another close friend or family member who you would not hold it against or think less of for being involved.

Now reread what you've written but this time it is your situation and you want to discuss it with a close friend or family member (someone not involved or connected with this situation in any way). Ask yourself "Would that individual hold this situation against me or think me any less of a person for being involved in it?" If you answered "no," go on to the next paragraph; if you answered "yes", choose another close friend or close family member who would not hold this against you (again, someone not connected in any way with the event you wrote down).

Finally reread what you've written once more and say to yourself, "I forgive myself for this," and mean it as best as you can at that moment. Fold up the sheet of paper, tear it up and throw it away immediately.

Practice Time: 1 minute/written event.

Indications: Releasing unproductive thoughts and emotions (such as guilt, anger, feelings of betrayal etc.) that we think are directed towards others, but are usually directed against ourselves. This is true whether we've been wronged by someone, or have wronged another.

Best Time To Use: The moment you realize you just said or did something regretful. Keep in mind that if it has taken a while to build up the emotions regarding the situation you want to be free of, you may need to per-form this procedure several times before enough of the emotions are released. This practice will allow you to feel comfortable again when recalling this incident. Forgiveness of self and others is a powerful skill in regaining health on all levels.

The Chinese have a saying, "One meter of thick ice does not melt in one day." This means that if you have been bothered by a situation for a long time, you've invested a good deal of emotional energy into it. The emotions and the regret surrounding this memory have become "solid" like an iceberg. Therefore, let the light and heat of forgiveness begin to melt away the solidness. Then, all you are left with is the memory and the opportunity to choose a better way of handling a similar situation in the future.

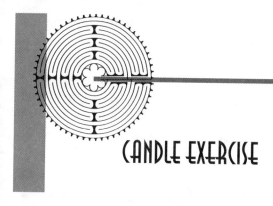

CHAPTER 5

CANDLE EXERCISE

Guiding Principle: The mind is only at rest when it focuses on a single thought or item.

Light a candle and place it on a tabletop about one foot in front of you. Gaze at the flame gently, as if you are watching the sails from sailboats as they lazily float on a lake near the horizon. Blink when you need to and breathe comfortably.

Practice Time: 1-5 minutes/session.

Indications: For general relaxation.

Best Time To Use: While taking a bath, listening to music and so on.

Candle Variation: If you want to develop better concentration, listening ability and memory skills:

Place a piece of paper on the table between you and the candle.

Purchase a silent, digital, battery operated egg timer and set it for 10 minutes.

Hold a pencil and place its point at the top left hand corner of the paper. Light the candle and start the timer.

Gaze gently at the flame. Each time your mind wanders from the flame put a small vertical hashmark on the paper and move the pencil point just to the right of that mark. Next gently put your attention back on the flame. Each time your attention wanders record a hashmark. Distractions can include: bodily itches, thinking about dinner, etc.

Do this exercise once a day for 10 minutes and over time, notice the improvement in your concentration, listening and memory skills!

Practice Time: 10 minutes/day.

Best Time To Use: Pick a time of day and stick to it as closely each day as possible.

NOTE: It is best when both candle techniques are performed in a room with some background lighting. Otherwise, a completely dark background behind the candle can lead to eye strain.

Indications: Attention Deficit Disorder, Tinnitus (ringing/buzzing in the ears), unsatisfactory listening skills, poor memory, difficulty visualizing or meditating, Anxiety and physical pain.

RAY'S RINGING

Ray, a 67-year-old Pharmacist, was suffering from Tinnitus (ringing in the ears.) This ringing became so disruptive to his work of filling prescriptions that he was scared of harming his customers by dispensing the wrong medication. He was taught to practice the Candle Variation technique and he did so daily for 10 minutes. Three months later, he reported that the ringing in his ears was as loud as ever, but he now had the ability to take his attention off of the ringing, direct his attention where he wanted it to go, and keep it there for as long as he chose. Ray proved the old axiom that "you are where your attention is at", and as he gratefully put it, "I guess you can teach an old dog new tricks!"

CHAPTER 6

PROGRESSIVE MUSCLE RELAXATION

Dr. Edmund Jacobson, Chicago 1929.

Guiding Principle: Anxiety-producing thoughts create muscular tension. Muscle tension leads to physical discomfort and irritability. Muscle relaxation reduces these conditions at their source.

Close your hand into a fist with no tension ("low tension") and perceive how your hand feels; now gently open your hand. Close your hand again and slowly tighten it to 50 percent of your strength ("medium tension") and perceive how that feels; now slowly open

19

your hand. Notice any difference in how your hand feels? Close your hand one last time and slowly bring the tension in your fist up to 100% of your strength; put your attention in your hand, notice what it feels like. Count slowly to 4 and take a big deep breath. Then slowly exhale as you simultaneously release the tension in your fist and gently open your hand.

You can tense and relax any muscle group in your body using this technique. For example, you can start at your toes and work your way up the body (or vice versa). Alternately, you can tense just the particular parts of your body that are tight, e.g. shoulders, thighs, etc.

Note: If an area of your body tends to go into spasm regularly, avoid doing this technique in that area. For example, many people experience spasms in the calf muscles; therefore, avoid tensing them. If you have a vascular condition like Retinopathy, (weakened blood vessels in the eyes) avoid applying this technique in the affected areas. Consult your doctor.

Practice Time: 5-10 minutes/session.

Indications: Tense, tired or sore muscles, feeling disconnected/out of touch with your body, Insomnia.

Best Time To Use: Before going to sleep and/or upon awakening, sitting, standing, or lying down (at work or at home), when thoughts are running rampant and other techniques have been ineffective.

A TOTAL RELAX

Stand with your feet shoulder width apart. Bring your arms straight out in front of your body at shoulder height, touching your palms together and bend your knees slightly ("starting position").

Take in a slow, big deep breath through your nose and simultaneously:

1. Bring both arms straight back into a "human cross" position.

2. Tense your entire body from low to medium to high tension (the highest point of tension will be when your arms are completely out to each side forming the "cross").

Hold your breath in this position for a few seconds, and then completely and forcefully exhale through your mouth. Simultaneously, release the tension in your body and bring your arms back to "starting" position as described above.

Note: While you are forcefully exhaling, imagine all the "stale and heavy" energy that surrounds you being pushed away from your body. Since nature abhors a vacuum, see bright and vibrant energy flowing in to fill the emptiness you have just created around your body. Feel it revive and strengthen you.

Practice Time: 30-60 seconds/session (3 or 4 breaths = 1 session).

Indications: Quick relief from the built up physical and mental tension of an excessively stressful situation.

Best Time To Use: When you are feeling very tense and/or out of control with strong emotions.

MENTAL MUSCLE RELAXATION

This is a variation for those of you who are not able to use Jacobson's method or A Total Relax for medical reasons.

Close your eyes. Imagine that you are at home in your favorite room, lounging barefoot on your favorite piece of furniture or on a soft carpet. The room is a bit on the cooler side, but still comfortable. See a person that you care about (and who cares about you) come into this room carrying a large bath towel that just came out of the dryer. This person brings the towel to you and lovingly wraps it around your bare feet. You immediately feel the warmth from the towel on your feet and you feel very secure in the warmth.

Now feel the warmth spread up to your calf muscles, letting these muscles relax within this warmth. That warm feeling moves up into your thighs and you notice your thigh muscles relaxing and letting go of any tension within that warmth. Now slowly bring that warm feeling up to your pelvis and buttocks, then, in turn, up into your abdomen and lower back, chest and upper back. Feel those tired muscles relax within the warmth.

Now bring that warm, nurturing feeling into your shoulders and down your upper arms, through your forearms and out your fingertips. Bring this warm feeling up into your neck and up around your mouth, nose, ears, and eyes. Finally, cause that warm feeling to move up over the top of your head to the back of your head, until your whole body is bathed in this safe and nurturing warmth and you feel very relaxed. When you are ready, take in a slow deep breath. When you exhale, open your eyes.

Practice Time: 1-3 minutes/session.

Indications: Fear, Anxiety, scattered thoughts, tired/sore/painful muscles, feeling disconnected/ out of touch with your body.

Best Time To Use: Anytime you have a quiet minute.

BONITA'S ANGER

Bonita, a 53-year-old Saleswoman for a large corporation, reported that her mood fluctuated from moment to moment, depending on how pleasant or frustrating her last phone call had been. She became enraged when the caller wasn't listening or acted rudely towards her. Bonita experienced this anger as vengeful thoughts toward the caller; she noticed that her neck, shoulders and upper back would tighten up. Taking a 5 minute break away from her desk would only leave her feeling the same when she returned. Then, Bonita was instructed how to perform "A Total Relax" either on the way to the bathroom at work or in one of the bathroom stalls. After using this technique several times within a few days, she found that her thoughts slowed down, her anger cleared and her neck, shoulder and back stiffness were significantly reduced. With more practice, Bonita became a calmer, happier and more capable sales person.

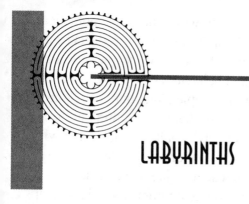

CHAPTER 7

LABYRINTHS

Labyrinths are tools that have been used by many cultures throughout history. Their function is to further those who are on the path to a more balanced spiritual, emotional, psychological and physical well being. A labyrinth has a single, winding, unobstructed path from the outside to the center, unlike a maze which has many dead ends and wrong choices designed to trick the mind. The labyrinth is often seen as a metaphor for one's spiritual "life" journey; many twists and turns but no dead ends. In other words, we always have the opportunity to make another choice in life or "turn" in the labyrinth.

27

When walking a labyrinth with others, a hypothetical "mirror" is often held up before you; it reflects back to you (through viewing other walkers) the beliefs, attitudes, perceptions and behaviors that you express daily. We are always meeting people along our "path" through life, and therefore, how we behave and think in these situations is re-created while walking a labyrinth with others. It is therefore an opportunity to learn more about yourself, and then choose to make those personal changes that can lead to having improved relationships, higher creativity and overall happiness.

The labyrinth is a powerful tool to help your mind and body relax. Anecdotal research by Dr. Wayne London indicates that labyrinths have a positive effect on brainwave activity and neurological response. The chance to release both mental and physical tension by walking or fingerwalking a labyrinth is there for each individual. In addition, those people who find it difficult to sit still and meditate or pray will find the perfect outlet in the walking meditation that is the labyrinth experience. It is simultaneously kinesthetic and introspective, a complete mind-body integrative activity.

People have used labyrinths as oracles; places to receive answers to life's troubling questions and an oasis for the spirit. In other words, a place to receive proper "nourishment" for the spirit within by connecting with a divine nature; a situation not readily available in our usual day to day existence. It is also a tool that bridges the ever-widening gap between traditional religious ritual and new age spiritual practices.

In sum, a labyrinth is a playground for allowing our intuitions to have free reign. So follow your head and hour heart while inside the "walls" of a labyrinth; what many consider to be "*Sacred Space*."

SUGGESTIONS FOR USING PAPER LABYRINTHS

Color in any of the 3 following labyrinth designs (*see pages 32, 33 and 34*) using crayons, colored pencils etc. Be sure to use the colors you find attractive, and use enough color variation to make it easy for your eyes to follow your finger as you trace the path.

Once you finish coloring the labyrinth pattern, choose a finger from either hand as your "walking" finger. Begin to make your breathing smooth.

Place your finger at the entrance of the labyrinth, and begin to trace the path to the center at the pace that feels right to you. You can enhance your experience by practicing one of the following activities.

1. Quiet your mind by focusing on your breath.

2. Pray for yourself or someone else.

3. Keep a question in mind making it feel "real" by tying your emotions into it.

When you reach the "center," pause and take several deep breaths. Release your prayer or question and remain there quietly, either with your finger in the center or with your hands comfortably in your lap. When you are ready to leave the center, (as if feeling "satisfied" after a good meal) retrace the path back out.

Practice Time: 30 seconds-5 minutes.

Indications: Attention Deficit Disorder, scattered thinking, Anxiety, Anger, Grief, feeling disconnected from a divine influence, seeking answers to questions.

Best Time To Use: Whenever you feel the need to leave your everyday experiences behind and enter a *"Sacred Space."*

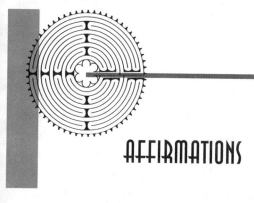

CHAPTER 8

AFFIRMATIONS

Guiding Principle: We all have internalized self-state-ments (such as "I am poor", "I am fat", "No one loves me" etc.), which at one time may have helped us break out of old patterns, but since have become an impedance to further growth and development. Consequently, these self-statements keep us from feeling happy and confident in situations where we naturally would, and lead to unnecessary stress. Our reality is shaped by these inter-nal statements.

Affirmations are self-statements that affirm your right as an individual to embrace and achieve the kinds of changes in yourself that you choose to make.

35

One way to use affirmations is to select a statement that depicts a personal philosophy or quality you would like to exhibit more often, such as, "I am a worthwhile individual, worthy of respect." Next write down your chosen statement in the middle of a sheet of paper. At the top of the paper, sign your name and fold the paper so that neither your name nor the statement is visible. Then, the first thing you do when you get up in the morning, and the last thing you do before going to sleep at night, is to read your name and the affirmation out loud.

Another way of using affirmations is to select a statement and repeat it to yourself whenever you need to be reminded of this change in attitude or philosophy.

Recommendation* Keep a journal of your day-to-day experiences when using an affirmation, to see how your reality changes with your practice.

Your affirmations might include:

I am learning to be optimistic and challenged by new experiences.

I am able to say no to others, knowing that my time is as important as anyone else's.

I am letting go of jealousy towards another person's successes.

I am able to lose 20 pounds.

I can achieve anything I set out to do.

I am gentle and kind and forgive myself.

I quickly release emotions about situations over which I have no control, and use my energy on those which are in my power to change.

I am learning that everyone and everything around me is my teacher.

I am confident in my ability to be successful in

_____.

I am using my strength, wisdom and experience to

_____.

Practice Time: 5-10 seconds/session.

    Indications: Desire to change thoughts, beliefs and ultimately the way the world responds to you.

Best Time To Use: Either twice per day or anytime you need the boost of reminding yourself of this new philosophy/quality you are building within yourself.

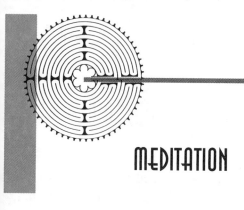

CHAPTER 9

MEDITATION

Guiding Principle: Our true nature is to be at peace.

There are many ways to meditate; as meditation is wed to no particular culture or religion. Three ways will be presented. For the intent of this book, meditation is a self-enrichment process which embraces the quieting of the body-mind system for the purpose of relaxation and inner awareness. For best results, meditation should at first be performed in a quiet area, preferably sitting up as lying down may induce sleep.

Begin by "watching" the natural rhythm of your breath enter and exit through your nostrils (a meditation in itself).

or:

Take 3-5 Abdominal Breaths to quiet yourself and prepare for meditation.

(HANTING "OM" OUT LOUD:

Mantras like "om" are sounds that contain their own vibrational rate. When introduced to the body, (which is itself a system of organs which vibrate at particular rates) these sounds can help balance various organs and energy systems in the body, and/or lead you into deeper and more satisfying states of relaxation.

Take in a series of big, comfortable deep breaths, and chant "om" out loud on each exhale. "Om" will then extend into the sound "oooommmmm." Make your chant loud enough to hear, and experiment by using different pitches. Notice parts of your mouth, nose, and throat vibrating during the chant. Upon finishing the chanting, remain breathless as long as is comfortable. You may also silently say this or another relaxing sound or word on or between each inhale and exhale (similar to the Relaxation Response.)

Practice time: 5 to 20 minutes/session.

Indications: Mental/physical fatigue, mild Depression, Anxiety, uncontrollable thoughts, hostility, High Blood Pressure, arrested personal development.

Best Time To Use: In a quiet place, pick 1 or 2 separate times each day to sit and gently repeat the mantra you've chosen.

Note: the above "practice time," "indications" and "best time to use" also apply to the following meditations.

LIGHT WITHIN THE HEART AREA:

Close your eyes and focus your attention on the center of your chest (at the height of your heart). With your imagination, create a brilliant light of any color emanating from this area. Endow this light with the characteristics you find morally and ethically valuable such as, honesty, compassion, love for all people and creatures, acceptance, willingness to forgive, service, etc. Recognize these qualities as gifts given to you by your God or Creator.

Once you have focused on this light for a short time, remove your attention from it and allow thoughts to parade by in the space behind your closed eyes. Watch a thought without judging it, then gently dismiss it by saying to yourself the word(s) "empty" or "empty out." Gently usher the thought out of your mind as if you were asking a friend to leave when he or she has inadvertently overstayed a welcome. As the thought leaves, gently notice this departure and focus on the quiet, thought-free field behind your closed eyes.

HERE & NOW MOMENT:

Sit quietly, eyes closed, and become aware of feeling yourself sitting in your chair, feeling the presence of someone sitting near you, hearing the sounds around you, smelling any scent in the air and noticing any taste in your mouth. This sensory awareness focuses your attention in the present moment. Then, open your eyes and look around. Notice objects without making judgements or putting labels on them (*pure observation*). All judgements and labels exist in the past. As such, they tend to block our perceptions of reality in the present. Misperceiving the present reality (because we have judged it to be identical to the past) can and often does lead to interpersonal conflicts and unnecessary emotions. If you find yourself labeling or judging, say to yourself "empty" or "empty out," thereby releasing the label or judgement and returning to a state of non-reactive, non-judging observation.

MATT'S HEART

Matt, a 42-year-old father of three, who had experienced a heart attack three weeks ago was looking for ways to lower his skyrocketing blood pressure. He did everything possible to avoid going on medication for this. Matt was then introduced to several meditations and found the "Light within The Heart Area" meditation the one most comfortable for him, as it best fit his personality and lifestyle. After a week of daily practice (for 5-10 minutes each day), Matt's family and co-workers noticed that he appeared calmer and was less likely to react to the "little things" that used to upset him. Two months later, when he saw his Cardiologist for follow up, his blood pressure was near enough to normal that his doctor did not require him to go on medication to lower his blood pressure. Matt has continued to practice meditation daily and remains off of this type of medication.

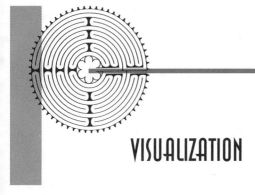

(HAPTER 10

VISUALIZATION

Guiding Principle: Creating body responses through use of mental images.

When you are sitting at the breakfast table on a Sunday morning preparing to partake in a pancake breakfast, what tells you that you are sitting there and not at your desk at work? Your 5 physical senses. In other words, the sight of your dining room gives your body clues as to where you are; you smell pancakes cooking, you hear sausage sizzling in the pan, and you feel yourself sitting on those distinctive chairs at the dining room table.

When the food is brought to your table, you taste the pancakes and sausages. Mmm...good. The total picture generated by your five physical senses now becomes your reality; you are sitting at the table eating delicious foods. This is how we perceive reality.

Now pretend that you are holding a whole lemon:

What does it look like?

How does it feel?

Now take an imaginary knife and cut it in half.

What does it smell like?

Squeeze it until juice squirts out.

What does it sound like?

Take a big bite of it.

What does it taste like?

You have now successfully experienced a lemon with all 5 of your "mental" physical senses. Just as at one point you experienced a real lemon with several of your physical senses, you have re-created the reality called "lemon" in your mind from memory. When the mind does this, the body does not recognize the difference between a recalled lemon and an actual one. I'll bet you proved that one to yourself earlier when you bit into the imaginary lemon. Your mouth physically puckered, didn't it!

This is why visualization works. For example, conjure up an image of yourself lying on a beach in Hawaii: smell the ocean air, see seagulls flying above the pristine, white sand, hear the waves as they thunder against craggy rocks at the shore-line, and feel the warm nurturing sand beneath you. If you go swimming in the ocean, you taste the harsh salt on your lips. Because of the way the mind-body connection works, your body benefits as if you really were on a beach in Hawaii. For example, muscle tension decreases, heart rate slows, blood pressure lowers and so forth.

Practice Time: 2-10 minutes/session.

 Indications: Mental and/or physical fatigue, emotional or physical tension, Anxiety, Insomnia, physical pain.

Best Time To Use: Anytime.

PHIL IN MAUI

Phil, a 23-year-old Construction Assistant and student, complained of sleepless nights, fatigue and generalized or free floating anxiety. He attended school on a partial grant, so if he performed below standard the grant would be withdrawn. Phil was constantly fearful of losing his grant money and thoughts of "not measuring up" kept him awake at night. However, he was trained in visualization, and when asked where he would like to travel in his imagination, Phil choose Maui. After a few nights of bedtime practice, Phil's fear had decreased to a manageable level so it was relatively easy for Phil to fall and stay asleep. Usually he was asleep before completing the visualization. Phil would awaken the next morning feeling refreshed.

THOUGHT STOPPING

Guiding Principle: Unwanted and unproductive thoughts may be arrested before they induce harmful emotional states and diminish physical or emotional health.

Sit or lie down and observe the thoughts passing through your mind. When you are ready, yell out loud (or silently to yourself) the word "stop!" Yell like you mean it. What happened to those thoughts? They stopped, didn't they? You now have a strong tool to quiet unwanted thoughts despite their intensities. The trick is to catch a thought early; once it's gone, immediately replace it with a desired or productive thought. For example, did you ever attempt to follow a diet or another discipline only then to battle counterproductive thoughts? I certainly have. These thoughts are very sneaky. They pop up at any time.

I remember years ago being part of a group that felt it important to develop mind-body discipline by devoting two days out of each week to eating only fruit. I was doing fine until one night when I was ravenous! I went to the freezer hoping to find some type of fruit. Instead, I found a quart of orange sherbet. Normally I wouldn't have given it a second look, but on this night I thought, "Well it's orange flavored, and orange is a fruit, therefore it's a fruit!" I grabbed the container and began to devour it, grateful for the good fortune of having such a tasty fruit in the house. After many scoops, reality hit . . . how could I have been taken in? As I began chastising myself, I remembered to yell "stop!" Afterward, the self-chastisement ceased. I then quickly added the productive thought "I have followed the discipline well up to this point, and it was only a small mistake to stray from my commitment. I will be watchful for this in the future." What a quick and easy stress reliever!

Practice Time: 5-10 seconds for each unwanted thought.

Indications: Anger, Anxiety, Fear, Obsessions, Guilt, Perseveration, Insomnia.

Best Time To Use: Whenever you experience thoughts that lead to strong, unwanted or unproductive emotions. The same holds true for undesirable behaviors.

ABOUT THE AUTHOR

Neal Harris is a Licensed Clinical Professional Counselor, with a Master's Degree in Applied Psychology. He is the director of Relax For Life, a wellness and holistic health consulting firm, and has presented seminars to corporations, hospitals, colleges, professional audiences and community groups since 1985. Topics include: relaxation and self-enrichment training, experiencing labyrinths, self esteem, exercise motivation, seated massage, goal setting, organizing space, the mind-body connection, meditation, and practical spirituality.

His exposure to, and training in various forms of relaxation, holistic health and self-development techniques have occurred in both the United States and India. Neal was also part of the first non-medical bodywork team invited to China to study Tuina, a form of Traditional Chinese Medicine and massage. He has taught Massage Therapy, and is a Reiki master-teacher, providing both Reiki therapy, and Reiki initiation classes.

Besides "Pocket Stress Manager", Neal is the author of a relaxation CD and audiotape. He is also the originator of the Earth-Wisdom Labyrinth located in Elgin, Illinois. This labyrinth is a huge outdoor rock structure, open to the public, and patterned after the famous cathedral labyrinth located in Chartres, France. Neal is the creator of traveling labyrinths, as well as kits for laying outdoor labyrinths. He is also the designer of unique finger labyrinths tools. He leads labyrinth classes for corporations, hospital programs, colleges and the general public.

Neal utilizes self-enrichment and spirituality coaching, light-assisted psychotherapy as well as his unique modality "labyrinth counseling" to assist people with a wide variety of issues. Anxiety, adjustment reactions, anger and mild depression are some examples. Additionally, he lends his expertise as a support group leader and private holistic counselor for those individuals who experience life-affirming conditions, such as diabetes, cancer and heart disease. His work with them explores integrative medical options as well as the psychology of illness and recovery.

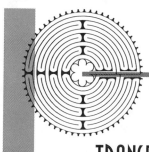

SUGGESTED READING LIST

TRANSFORMATIONAL:

Be As You Are: The Teachings of Sri Ramana Maharshi.
D. Goodman, Arkana Books, 1990.

Conversations With God.
N. Walsh, G.P. Putnam's Sons, 1995.

Grist For The Mill.
Ram Dass, Unity Press, 1977.

Labyrinths: What Are They?
Prehistory to the 21st Century
K. Torrez, Labyrinths Unlimited, 1994.

TRANSFORMATIONAL *(Continued)*

Love Is Letting Go Of Fear.
G. Jampolsky, Celestial Arts, 1979.

Man's Search For Meaning.
V. Frenkl, Simon & Schuster, 1984.

Mazes & Labyrinths.
W.H. Matthews, Dover Publications, 1970.

On Having No Head:
A Contribution To Zen In The West.
D. Harding, The Buddhist Society, 1961.

Plunge Into Eternity:
An Interview With H.W.L. Poonja.
C. Ingram, Yoga Journal, September/October 1992,
pp. 56-63.

Prior To Consciousness:
Talks With Sri Nisargadatta Maharaj.
J. Dunn, Acorn Press, 1985.

Reiki: A Torch In Daylight.
K. Mitchell, Mind Rivers Publications, 1994.

TRANSFORMATIONAL *(Continued)*

The Road Less Traveled.
M. Peck, Simon & Schuster, 1978.

Wake Up & Roar: Satsang With H.W.L. Poonja.
Pacific Center Publishing, 1992.

Walking A Sacred Path.
L. Artress, Riverhead Books, 1995.

HEALING:

A Manual Of Self Healing.
E. Shattock, Destiny Books, 1982.

An Alternative Approach To Allergies.
T. Randolph & R. Moss, Harper & Row, 1979.

The Art Of Aromatherapy.
R. Tisserand, Destiny Books, 1977

Bach Flower Therapy:
Theory & Practice. M. Scheffer, Healing Arts Press, 1984.

HEALING: *(Continued)*

Edgar Cayce: Encyclopedia Of Healing.
R. Karp, Warner Books, 1986.

How To Live Between Office Visits.
 B. Siegel, Harper/Collins, 1993.

Human Energy Systems.
J. Schwartz, E.P. Dutton, 1980.

Love, Medicine & Miracles.
B. Siegel, Harper & Row, 1986.

Medical Divination.
H. Tomlinson, Garden City Press, 1966.

My Search For Radionic Truths.
R. Denning, JFB Printing, 1981.

The Official Reiki Handbook.
 B. Ray, Y. Carrington,
American International Reiki Association, 1982.

Peace, Love & Healing.
B. Siegel, Harper & Row, 1989.

HEALING: *(Continued)*

Progressive Relaxation.
E. Jacobson, University Of Chicago Press, 1974.

Quantum Healing: Exploring The Frontiers Of Mind/Body Medicine.
D. Chopra, Bantam Books, 1990.

The Relaxation & Stress Reduction Workbook.
M. Davis, E. Eschelman, M. McKay,
New Harbinger Publications, 1990.

Vibrations:
Healing Through Color, Homeopathy & Radionics.
V. Macivor & S. LaForest, Samuel Weiser Inc., 1990.

PSYCHOLOGICAL/METAPHYSICAL:

A Book Of Angels.
S. Burnham, Ballantine Books, 1990.

The Ancient Wisdom.
A. Besant, Theosophical Publishing House, 1983.

PSYCHOLOGICAL/METAPHYSICAL *(Continued)*

After We Die, What Then?
George Meeks, (no date).

A World Beyond.
R. Montgomery, Fawcett Crest, 1971.

Dianetics: The Modern Science Of Mental Health.
L. Hubbard, Bridge Publications, 1986.

The Existential Imagination.
F. Karl, & L. Hamalian, Fawcett Publications, 1963.

Jonathan Livingston Seagull.
R. Bach, Avon Books, 1973.

The Kin Of Ata Are Waiting For You.
D. Bryant, Random House, 1971.

Mechanics Of Dreams.
J. Rothermel, SOM Publishing, 1989.

Move Ahead With Possibility Thinking.
R. Schuller, Doubleday & Co., 1967.

BIOGRAPHIES:

Footprints Of Guatama The Buddha.
M. Byles, Quest Books, 1957.

The Guru.
M. Hall, Phylosophical Research Society, 1944.

Joy's Way.
B. Joy, St. Martin's Press, 1979.

Return Of The Rishi.
D. Chopra, Houghton Mifflin Co., 1988.

Self-Realization: Life & Teachings Of Bhagavan Sri Ramana Maharshi.
B. Narasimhaswami, Niranjananda Swamy, 1944.

The Eagle & The Rose.
R. Altea, Warner Books, 1995.

ORACLES:

Celestine Prophesy.
J. Redfield, Satori Press, 1993.

Crystal Stair.
E. Klein, Oughten House Publications, 1990.

The I Ching (*Chinese Book Of Changes*).
R. Wilhelm & C. Baynes, Princeton University Press, 1971.

Wisdomkeepers:
Meetings With Native American Spiritual Elders.
S. Wall & H. Arden, Beyond Words Publishing (no date).

Mutant Messages Down Under.
M. Morgan, Harper Collins, 1991.

Other Council Fires Were Here Before Ours.
J. Sams & T. Nitsch, Harper Collins, 1991.